The ABC's of Being a Good Friend

Emily Ashcraft

WestBow Press books may be ordered through booksellers or by contacting:

WestBow Press
A Division of Thomas Nelson & Zondervan
1663 Liberty Drive
Bloomington, IN 47403
www.westbowpress.com
844-714-3454

Because of the dynamic nature of the Internet, any web addresses or links contained in this book may have changed since publication and may no longer be valid. The views expressed in this work are solely those of the author and do not necessarily reflect the views of the publisher, and the publisher hereby disclaims any responsibility for them.

Any people depicted in stock imagery provided by Getty Images are models, and such images are being used for illustrative purposes only.
Certain stock imagery © Getty Images.

Illustrated by: Daniel Majan

ISBN: 978-1-6642-6499-1 (sc)
ISBN: 978-1-6642-6501-1 (hc)
ISBN: 978-1-6642-6500-4 (e)

Library of Congress Control Number: 2022907709

Print information available on the last page.

WestBow Press rev. date: 5/23/2022

WESTBOW
P R E S S®
A DIVISION OF THOMAS NELSON
& ZONDERVAN

The ABC's of Being a Good Friend

Teacher, **what is a good friend?**" I often hear asked.
To describe a good friend is no short simple task.
Friends come in all ages and types, it is true,
But good friends at their core will be true to YOU.

So come, take a look, at this ABC book,
and I'm sure you will discover,
that the best type of friend is forgiving and fair,
they won't judge a book by its cover.

And after you read, I'm sure you will see,
good friends are worth hanging onto.
Do you have a good friend?
I hope that you do.
And when your friend is asked what a good friend looks like,
I'm hoping that they'll point to you.

The ABC's of a Good Friend

3

Good friends are **A**ccepting.

They really don't care, 'bout your weight
or your height or the color of your hair.
They care about YOU, the real person inside.
Who you are isn't something you should have to hide.
Accepting*: Someone who is accepting treats others like they belong.*

Good friends are **B**rave.

They welcome a challenge with a smile on their face.
They're determined and willing to finish each race.
And if they get scared or tired or worried,
I know that you'll notice and come in a hurry.
Brave*: Someone who is brave is courageous, not afraid.*

Good friends are **C**aring.

When you need to talk, you know they'll be there.
If you're anxious or nervous they will be aware.
They'll bring you some yummies, they'll encourage you.
If you need to hear truth, they will tell you that too.
*Caring: Someone who is caring shows
kindness and concern for other people.*

Good friends are **D**ependable.

They're true blue!
When trouble comes up they'll be there to help you.
And when they're in a jam, I know you'll help them too.
*Dependable: Someone who is dependable can be trusted;
they do what they say they will do.*
*True Blue: Just like the sky is always blue (even though clouds
cover it up sometimes) good friends will always be there.*

Good friends are **E**njoyable.

They make you smile!
Whether you've known them a short time or a good long while.
Friends bring adventures and giggles and fun!
They make you laugh with funny faces and puns.
Enjoyable: *Someone who is enjoyable is fun to be around.*

Good friends are **F**orgiving.

We all make mistakes!
If you hurt their feelings, I know you will take,
the time to apologize and make things right.
Good friends say "I'm sorry" if they have a fight.
Forgive: *To forgive is to let go of being angry at someone.*

Good friends are **G**ifted.

They ALL have great skills.
Those skills might be painting or basketball drills.
Some friends may love running or singing or math!
Every friend has great gifts and will walk their own path.
Gifted: *Someone who is gifted has great skills at something.*

Good friends are **H**onest.

They say what is true.
If they make a mistake, then they will tell you.
Good friends don't tell lies, whether big or small.
They know that your trust is worth more than it all.
Honest: *Someone who is honest tells the truth.*

Good friends are Inspiring.

They drive you to GO.
They dream big and work hard because they know,
the friends you spend time with impact who you are.
They want to support you and help you go far.
*Inspiring: Someone who is inspiring causes other people
to want to work hard or do great things.*

Good friends are NOT Jealous.

This means they're ok,
if you want to include other friends when you play.
They welcome newcomers!
They know in the end,
you won't ever lose when you gain a new friend.
*Jealous: Jealousy means an angry feeling that wants what
other people have. Good friends aren't angry or jealous.*

Good friends are **K**ind to people and things.

This means that they share and are always caring.
They take out the garbage, they help in a storm.
A person who's kind will be friendly and warm.
Kind: Someone who is kind is gentle and enjoys helping others.

Good friends are **L**oyal.

They know you're not perfect.
But through your mistakes, they know you're still worth it.
Friends who are loyal are faithful and true.
They always forgive and they know you will too.
Loyal: Someone who is loyal is supportive all the time.

Good friends are NOT **M**ean.

They aren't nasty or rude.
When you're hurting or sad, they'll be there for you.
Friends that are mean are not real friends at all.
Friends that are real help you up when you fall.
Mean: *Someone who is mean is not kind to people.*
Good friends are kind.

Good friends are **N**eeded.

Don't live life alone!
Talk to a friend, at school or by phone.
People need people to live life fully.
People need friends like peanut butter needs jelly.
Needed: *Someone who is needed is very important*
or necessary to someone else.

17

Good friends are **O**utstanding.

They're cream of the crop!
Their kindness and joy make them rise to the top.
An outstanding friend tries to put others first.
They comfort and calm you when you feel your worst.
Outstanding: Someone who is outstanding is
excellent, wonderful, the best of the best.
Cream of the crop*: For farmers, the cream of the crop means*
the best of the harvest. When we say friends are the cream
of the crop, it means they are the best friends around.

Good friends are **P**atient.

This means that they're careful.
They know that the words they say are powerful.
So when they get angry, they don't scream or shout.
They wait 'til they're calm and then work it out.
Patient: Someone who is able to stay calm and wait for
something or deal kindly with a difficult situation.

18

Good friends DON'T **Q**uit.

They finish what they start,
whether its math or chores or art.
Good friends persevere, that means 'stick things through.'
They'll never give up, on a job or on you.
*Quit: Someone who quits stops in the middle or leaves
a job unfinished. Good friends don't quit.*

Good friends are **R**espectful.

They say "Thank you" and "please."
Oh, "excuse me" too, they remember all these!
But more than just manners,
I think that you'll find,
that being respectful just means being kind.
*Respectful: Someone who is respectful understands that people and
things have value and should be treated with kindness and care.*

Good friends are **S**incere.
If they said it, they meant it.
They don't change who they are so the cool kids will buy it.
Being sincere is like being honest.
When good friends are sincere, you know they'll keep a promise.
*Sincere: Someone who is sincere acts in a
genuine and honest way all the time.*

Good friends are **T**rustworthy.
This means that you can,
share with them what's on your mind or your plans.
Friends who are trustworthy make wise decisions.
Friends who are trustworthy take time to listen.
*Trustworthy: If someone is trustworthy, you can rely on them to
do the right thing.*

23

Good friends are **U**nique.

Each is one of a kind!
Every person is different, but I think you will find,
that our differences can help each other to shine!
That's why your best friend may look different than mine.
Unique: Someone who is special and unlike anyone else.
Guess what? That's EVERYONE!
You are the only YOU, perfectly special and unique!

Good friends are **V**aluable, more than money or fame.

Those things go away, but good friends stay the same.
So don't put your trust in the things that will fade.
True friendships are treasures that last for decades.
Valuable: Something or someone who is worth a lot.
EVERY person is valuable.

Good friends are **W**orthy of your time and your trust.

When life brings you changes, you both will adjust.
Through days that feel sunny and days that feel gray,
friends that are worthy are friends that will stay,
whether they're minutes or miles away.
*Worthy: Someone or something that deserves
attention, praise, and respect.*

Good friends are e**X**amples.

This word you may know!
An example is something or someone you follow.
Good friends are examples of kindness and trust.
They know that doing the right thing is a must.
Example: Someone or something that should be imitated.

Good friends can be **Y**oung, or they can be old.

They can be quirky, they can be bold.
No matter their age one great truth must be told:
Friends that are real are worth their weight in gold.
Young: *Someone who is an early stage of life, like you!*

Good friends are **Z**any.

This means creative and fun!
They're full of ideas, and they get the job done.
They think big thoughts and they dream big dreams,
And when you help them out, you two make the best team.
Zany: *Someone who is zany is silly, wacky, interesting and fun!*

29

And so, dear one, we have come to the end.
You've learned so many ways to describe a good friend.

Which one is your favorite?
Which words are brand new?
Which ones would your good friends say about *you?*

"But teacher," you might say, "Oh what do I do?
I have not been a good friend, a friend who is true.
I've said some mean things and I've made some mistakes.
My mess-ups are more than my good friends can take."

Well, good friends are forgiving, remember that part?
If you change your ways you can have a fresh start.
Nobody's perfect, but I want you to know,
Friends who are true give you freedom to grow.

Printed in the United States
by Baker & Taylor Publisher Services